Latibule

Cara Critchley

BookLeaf
Publishing

India | USA | UK

Latibule © 2021 Cara Critchley

All rights reserved.

No part of this publication may be reproduced, stored in a retrieval system, or transmitted, in any form or by any means, electronic, mechanical, photocopying, recording or otherwise, without the prior written permission of the presenters.

Cara Critchley asserts the moral right to be identified as author of this work.

Presentation by *BookLeaf Publishing*

Web: www.bookleafpub.com

E-mail: info@bookleafpub.com

ISBN: 978-93-5761-216-6

First edition 2021

DEDICATION

To my friends and family, but most importantly,
my Ma & Grandy, who never fail to make me
feel important. I love you.

ACKNOWLEDGEMENT

Massive thank you's to my friends who had to endure random pieces of poetry and demands for their opinions - I couldn't have done this without you.

PREFACE

Hello! If you're reading this, then it means I've actually managed to publish something and that's so cool! Thank you for opening my book. I really appreciate it.

These poems are a random collection of poems in varying formats, genres and writing styles, yet are all by me. Honestly, some are downright depressing and others are so, so random. It's a lucky dip!

I hope you enjoy them as much as I enjoyed writing them.

Throne

there will not be a day where it is peaceful
for mankind knows no such thing
we started fighting over an apple
it is unknown how we are to end
but it won't be laughing
or dancing
unless on our enemies graves.

faith, trust and pixie dust
may as well be our future
far more likely than no more wars
even after years go by
and we wonder
why don't we just change already?

we will not rule the world
as there is a singular throne
and agreement isn't something we do
without back stabbings and politics
the result being the next generation who suffers.

the children who are so optimistic
they are eager to learn and grow up
but darling please,
stay little and stay small
for when you are big and tall
your voice won't matter any more
than it did before.

Night Owls

I often sit and wonder
that if the early bird catches the worm,
not that this is something I usually ponder,
but it'd be nice for someone to affirm,
that the sleepy birds don't fall under
the world's radar.

The sun sits and screams in the sky
whilst the moon runs away with fright at the
day's first light,
and I wonder why,
the world doesn't put up more of a fight,
I assume it's too much of a plight.

Night owls are a different breed
than those who rise before dawn
the very idea makes them want to bleed,
all whilst stifling a yawn.

A day is full of new adventures
to all who want to explore,
there are many places to venture
except for those who prefer to snore.

Here's to the sleepers
the dreamers and the believers,
may you rest as much as you content,
as sleeping is time well spent.

Try

i remember when it began,
the encompassing darkness deep in my gut.
it chased me no matter how far I ran,
appearing in every shadow, mirror and dream
but
only I could see it.

the long nights felt as wide as the world
and sandman went on strike
because all I could do was nothing but curl
into a ball so small
and hope to hell that I won't wake up at all.

Their world didn't stop when mine cracked
as I was one of many with deep blue insides
a swirling, bubbling and rancid sea of
powerlessness
It embodied, it devoured and it buried me whole.

Shovel in hand and words gone missing,
I tried so hard to rinse my heart out
To get rid of everything people kept dismissing
When a torch was lit and shone down below,

"Hey! Are you okay?"

"No, I'm not."

Whirling, swirling words said so plain
Yet how would I know they'd work all the same
because people will listen when you talk back
The string of silence is cut, severed and eroded.

Time slows down to a comforting pace,
No longer scary when it doesn't feel like a race,
And I can breathe at last,
That encompassing darkness doesn't feel so
heavy,
the mirrors show me stood proudly,
Shouting at the shadow to leave already
Because as much as it still hurts,
I can hold my voice steady,
and know that that torch will shine,
no matter how long I have to try.

I Do

Shrill shrieks fill the air, heads turning left and
right
The day is sweet, fresh and dry
Great white clouds enjoy their time in the sky
Even birds above pause in their flight,
What was the noise all about?
It appeared as though not very far out,
A man had gotten down on one knee,
Ring in hand for bride to be;
Her mouth open wide when she shouted without
a doubt –

"Yes!" So eager, so loud and excited was thee,
To decide her fate in the twelfth decree.
Now he, the one on the ground, went pastel and
faded,
Perhaps seeing his future all set out in front of
him, painted
A life so different than the one he had just
publicly traded.

Cautionary

This is a cautionary tale,
One full of organised chaos.
It begins on a minor scale,
A predator looking for someone to prey on,
And finding a victim quite frail.
His story is no more brawn than brain,
Barely left land to set sail,
When the sky opened and began to heavily rain.
There was a moment of panic of becoming a
folktale,
Nothing more than a story of disdain,
Drowned by a blue wave and,
No chance to explain
Just how much he wished he'd held his mothers
hand,
To tell her that her love hadn't been in vain.
However, then he felt sand beneath his
fingertips;
It wasn't followed by anything sharp or scary.
Prayers of thanks left his lips
Whilst he looked around his new world of
solitary.

Love

Love is taught and molded,
Expectations forged from parents,
Influenced by films, books and media.
Some know love as a wonderful thing;
It is full of joy, something to wait for.
Others know its alternative realm,
How people can hear but not listen,
Love is nothing against anger and shame
Because promises get broken when a fist is
raised.
A fair few know the reality
It's what you want it to be.
The key is comprehension and balance,
Not contention and authority,
Teach children humility, to care and share.
Before generations despair at the idea of forever.

Stranger

To the man who should've loved me,
I ask that you show them your best side
In my presence it was too much of you to be
But they should look at you clear-eyed,
With not a doubt in the world that you are kind.

To the man who should've loved me,
I remember when i was a part of your world,
Back when you were so proud of what I could
be
Though I'm sure all that pride is somewhere
hurled,
Where you can pretend I never even existed.

To the man who should've loved me,
It used to burn so bad,
This aching in my chest that screams worthless
That the years have dulled and become
armour-clad
Because I too have moved on, and become hurt
less.

To the man I loved,
We no longer communicate
And for that I am glad
That i have stopped chasing your bait,
Before you ruined any chance I had.

Labels

We spend our lives with labels on our backs
Designated by people or self identified,
They twist, stick and plaster to leave no gaps
Until you are an alias just to get by,
Try to be unique, an individual and not an
overlap
Identities shouldn't be something we hide
Not a 'perhaps' but a fight back,
To claim yourself in a court where you testified
That you are you and that's that,
It isn't a crime to have some pride.

Master of Machine

Because reason has to win,
I am sure we will come through.
It can't be the same as it has been
unless we get a fat screw
you, not that I would expect unseen
angels to take pity out of the blue
but it's been this way since nineteen.
Running out of ways to make do,
God, master of machine
If only, if only you knew
that our last hope was gasoline
and making the world burn too.

Fickle

Trust is such a fickle thing
There was so much I didn't know
I remember when you held me by a string,
It took years before your cracks began to show,
An ego desperately fighting against a coil
spring.
The floor turned to eggshells and steps became a
tiptoe
But it took nothing before you forced me into a
boxing ring.

– the ache in my heart and the taint of my
thoughts,
It was blinding and wound up through the bones
of my ribcage,
I don't know how I could have been so blind to
your unkind
Mocked for reasons so ignorant and ill-defined
That it was no surprise hate became entwined
Entwined into my very being, enveloped my
young mind
To try and protect myself against your bets and
threats,
I'm sorry I wasn't better, I'm sorry I wasn't
good enough for you.

The shame in my stomach, regretting ever
getting up and yet,
You acted like you hadn't a clue why I was so
blue.

Spite felt fresh in my veins when friends cut
your cords,
At least I wasn't to blame this time,
Because someone else had rang the alarm
And realized how you'd played your cards
Your face now plastered on every wall,
A warning calling out your crimes of bullying.

I hope you never know how it felt to be so raw,
An opened wound that couldn't heal
I hope you never know what I had saw,
When I looked in the mirror, my achille's heel.
I hope you stopped your games,
And calling people names.
I hope.

Chronic

A cursed palace calls my body home,
Where a temple should stand proudly
But those walls crumbled and fell
Replaced by aches and tiredness.
It is foreign, this body of mine
I am the migrant, clinging hold
Begging people to believe me when i claim
That I am the imposter, the stranger, the sham.
I do not belong in this shell of a facade
Because it looks like me but does not feel like
me,
My mouth feels robotic and mind too dark,
Looking out through eyes too blue.

Excuses replace questions of this condition,
They sound jumbled to my ears and i can't,
I can't accept the lies pinned to me.
Tests, tests and more tests - will it ever end?
I am tied to a spintop and rolled away,
Shouts of pleas meeting deaf ears
Because I don't look as I feel.

Fragile

there is a breaking point to me,
it may be closer than most
but it is valid and it is mine.
i am a box labelled 'fragile',
and my heart is founded by bubble wrap
because everyday is a battle to stay whole.
when you throw your words so sharp,
i cannot help my fearful tact
how do i act when i know you have me trapped?
there are no rulebooks to follow
no step-by-step guides,
so i trip and i stumble through
trying my best to get by,
without a clue what to do.

Robots

We are often described as robots,
Though i am not quite sure why
Because stereotypes get tied up in knots
When our actions don't comply.
Emotions we feel very much
Even if they are hard to understand
And ask before you touch,
Or you might find out firsthand,
Just how individual we are,
Rather than words on a page.
This is not to say we are always different,
sometimes you never know who is
And who isn't labelled or proud.
Whatever the case please think twice,
Before you compare a person to a mechanical
device.

Blank Pages

My favourite days are those of blank pages.
Pen or fingers stilled over paper and keys,
Waiting for inspiration to break free
But it also means no bad days and events,
Nothing but dull, empty thoughts
Useless though welcomed, even so
I crave the ability to write the good
Yet words only come with negativity
And those days, I hate them the most.

Nova

The way you look at me with eyes so bright,
It tugs at my heartstrings
And is nothing short of a delight
Because I know what you can bring.

Long walks with you by my side,
No complaints or dragging feet,
You have more energy than I can beat
But you'll still gladly stop and match my stride.

Loyalty that doesn't waver,
A reliance of devotion,
Even if it is not deserved,
Your love could match an ocean.

Some think it's strange,
You have taken over my life
But it is definitely worth the change
Because you, my friend, take away all my strife.

Holy Figures

forsaken ground trembles in wait,
thou must not take fright and turn;
whilst holy figures stand up to plate.

upon this earth we walk with no idea of date,
just readying for eternal burn;
forsaken ground trembles in wait.

spending our days wrapped in hate,
will we ever begin to try and learn;
whilst holy figures stand up to plate.

lives are ruled by whom has the power to
dictate,
yet to rebel is always yearned;
forsaken ground trembles in wait.

it is not to say if we will ever understand our
fate,
as thy kind thinks themselves all eterne;
whilst holy figures stand up to plate.

nevertheless, it approaches fast, never late,
prepared nor unaware, it is not to be discerned,
forsaken ground trembles in wait,
whilst holy figures stand up to plate.

Empty

There comes a time when you run out of words,
It is inevitable and expected but not easy
Your voice is not even a whisper as you strain to
be heard
The world continues to move swiftly with no
pause
It begs the question as to whether they listened
in the first place
Or if you've spent your days speaking to a sea of
nowt.
No matter how hard you try to think of
something clever,
Something funny or about the weather,
Nothing leaves the once safe haven of your
throat
As it becomes a cemetery for your hopes,
Your dreams and fears, whatever there may be,
It is no longer something that's free.

Trap

it billows as a vapour mapping its tracks,
unforgiving portals to a world unseen
yet felt so real, panic and dependency,
common but tainted in conversation;
beautified in waves of denial and so,
crusades of faith try to explain
why kids so innocent fall into its trap.
remedy after remedy, talking for days,
sleep so disrupted and appetites lost
months slip by as their minds decay
but they say they're okay because hey,
nobody sees it anyway.

Middle

It is surprising that after all this time,
That I am not yet tired of the climb
So I thrive, like ivy evergreen;
Slow growing but intricate, i will stampede
Leaving a bedraggled trail in my wake.
The fight is not over because it does not stop,
I am full of vitality, churning with unknown
mistakes;
Don't look back on fault or it will grind to a halt
And I, we, you, us, are more than a pass.

Stare

he lays there as we stand
waiting for a bus and avoiding his form
His coat is pulled over his upper body
As he tries to get off the cold, wet ground
By sleeping on a plastic bag.
His own backpack is clutched under his
head
And we hide our possessions as if any
moment,
He is going to jump up like a rapid dog
And attack.

I wonder if he's hungry,
I know he is cold.
It's before eight a.m and here he lays,
a display at a zoo despite no cages
I want to help but they stare,
I cannot toe the line of society
Alcohol, drugs, homeless,
We assume off the bat and heck,
I hope none of us end up like that.

Body

my hands tremble when i stare,
identical blues seeing right through
my facade so carefully crafted,
and it fractures every time.

the sight of me is a cross to bare,
as thoughts flood, hoping they are all untrue
the best word to mind is contorted
but i know the mirror does not define me.

even though it is hard to find,
i dig and i dig until i reach it,
past the manipulative messages of mine,
before there is beauty on my skin.

for once, i do not hate that i am undisguised
because it inches closer with childlike wonder,
helps itself to burrow in, safe at home, warm
within

i cradle it close, once foregin and forgotten.

my hands remain still, sure and sturdy.
i study the glass and smile so wide,
standing boldly, worthy and blooming,
claiming the love for my body,
for being unapologetically itself.

www.ingramcontent.com/pod-product-compliance
Lightning Source LLC
LaVergne TN
LVHW051243200726
843510LV00011B/1674